HOW DO WE KNOW
EINSTEIN WAS RIGHT?

JAMES MUIRDEN

SIMON & SCHUSTER
YOUNG BOOKS

First published in 1994 by
Simon & Schuster Young Books

© 1994 Simon & Schuster Young Books

Simon & Schuster Young Books
Campus 400
Maylands Avenue
Hemel Hempstead
Hertfordshire
HP2 7EZ

A CIP catalogue record for this book is available from the British
Library
ISBN 0 7500 1 521 7

Commissioning Editor: Tom Keegan
Designer: Simon Borrough
Editor: Kate Scarborough
Illustrators:
Steve Roberts,
Robert Holder (Beehive Illustration)

Picture acknowledgements

Bridgeman Art Library 23 bottom, 32; Cassell & Co 26;
Mary Evans Picture Library 8, 10 18; Fotomas 28; Michael Holford 25;
Hulton Deutsch 25 bottom; Ann Ronan 24, 25tl, 36; Scala 10;
Science Photo Library 15, 16, 19, 22, 23, 25tr, 35, 37, 41, 43 top; Zefa 43

Typeset by Goodfellow & Egan, Cambridge
Printed and bound in Hong Kong

Contents

About the Universe?

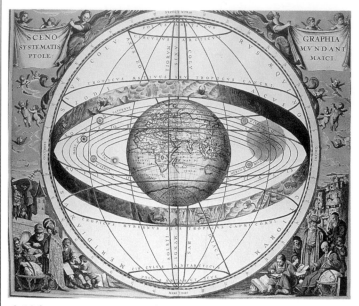

A 16th century representation of Ptolemy's model of the Universe

Two thousand years ago, the picture shown here (left) would have represented the Universe. People then believed that the Earth was at the centre of the Universe, with the Sun, Moon, planets and stars revolving round it. However, do we really know about the Universe even now?

At that time, people believed that the positions of the planets in the sky influenced events on the Earth. They studied their movements so that they could predict their future appearance. The astronomer Ptolemy's model of the Universe (left) was worked out about AD 150. Its accuracy was not questioned for about 1500 years, but it was completely wrong.

Kepler's theory

In 1601, Johannes Kepler came up with a new model. He worked out the planets' positions in the sky, assuming that the Earth and planets orbit the Sun in *elliptical* paths. The result was much more accurate than Ptolemy's theory.

A planet in an elliptical orbit moves faster when it is nearer the Sun. It moves from A to B in the same time it takes to move from C to D

Shapes in the stars

The star patterns, or constellations, were an important part of our progress towards a better understanding of the Universe. It was discovered that these patterns do not change over hundreds of years. This meant that there was a basic difference between the stars and the five planets or 'wandering stars' that are visible with the naked eye.

The brightest stars are named in records dating back to about 3000 BC, found in the Middle East. By about 800 BC some of the constellations recognised today had been named. Altogether there are 88 constellations in the whole sky.

Signs of the Zodiac
The Sun, Moon and planets move around a narrow band of the sky called the Zodiac. Leo is one of the 12 constellations forming the Zodiac.

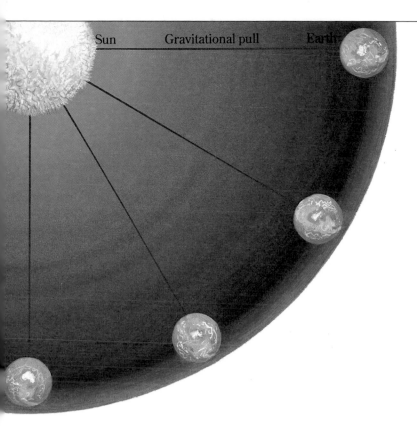

Sun   Gravitational pull   Earth

Universal gravity

Newton published his theory of *gravity* in 1687. He proposed that every object in the Universe contains a force that attracts other objects towards it. The more material in the body (the more massive it is) the stronger the force. The Sun's very powerful force of gravity holds the much smaller planets in orbit around it.

Relativity and the Universe

Einstein's general theory of relativity (1915) explains the strange effects of the speed of light. He proposed a 'thought experiment', since it could not be done in practice. A light flashes inside a very fast-moving truck. To an observer inside the truck it hits the front and back walls at the same instant. But to an observer outside the truck, it seems to hit the rear wall first because of the truck's speed.

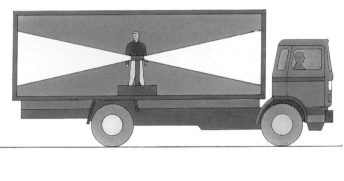

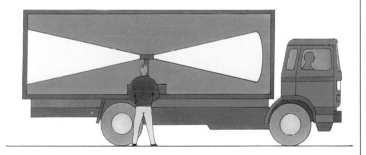

Distance, light and speed

In 1887 two physicists named Edward Morley and Albert Michelson set up an experiment. Light moves at about 300,000 km/s; the Earth moves in its orbit around the Sun at about 30 km/s. Logically, a beam of light projected in the same direction as the Earth should be moving 30 km/s faster, and one projected in the opposite direction should be moving 30 km/s slower. However, both beams still moved at 300 km/s!

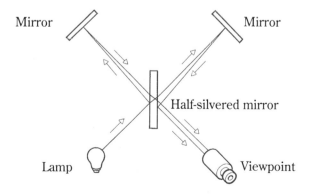

Light from the same lamp was split into two beams at right angles to each other. Both beams were discovered to travel at the same speed

Are they right?

Newton's theory of gravity makes sense to us because we can feel the effects of gravity around us all the time. The theory of relativity does not "make sense" because we are not familiar with objects travelling near the speed of light. However, astronomers studying the Universe often have to consider the speed of light, as you will discover.

Newton's theory of gravity explains the appearance of slow-moving objects such as planets perfectly well. Einstein's theory of relativity explains the appearance of fast-moving objects. But is Einstein right? Will future discoveries need new theories to explain them?

When the Earth began?

Everywhere we look, we see evidence of change. Seasons change, rivers alter their course, volcanoes throw up lava – even whole continents slowly move. In addition, living things have evolved. We are used to seeing *evolution* all around us.

But evolution is a recent idea. Until the 18th century, people thought that the Earth and Universe were created looking more or less as they are now. In 1745 the French scientist Georges-Louis

Leclerc Buffon suggested that the planets were formed from material ejected from the Sun at least 75,000 years ago.

In the 19th century, fossils showed that evolution of life forms must have been going on for far longer than 75,000 years. However, the idea of an evolving Earth did not become popular until Darwin's study of animals and plants showed that the evolution of life forms to their present state must have taken hundreds of millions of years.

Crust

Mantle

Outer Core

Inner Core

Earth's structure
The Earth was built up about 4.6 billion years ago when particles of rock and metal slammed together, forming a *molten* ball. The metal (mostly iron and nickel) sank to the centre because it was heavier than the rock. The solid crust floats on the molten upper mantle.

CHARLES DARWIN
Living things usually produce offspring that are slightly different from themselves. These variations may survive and prosper to produce a new and stronger species. He made these drawings of three types of finch he found in the Galapagos Islands, with different beaks that suit different kinds of habitat.

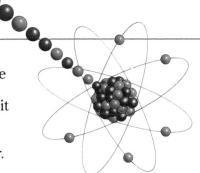

The age of the Sun

Darwin's long time-scale did not fit in with other evidence. For example, it was assumed that the Sun is at least as old as the Earth, or even older. In 1854 the German *physicist* Hermann Helmholtz proposed that the Sun was steadily shrinking, so that the gas inside became more and more *compressed*, giving out heat. However, the Sun could not have been shrinking for more than about 20 million years.

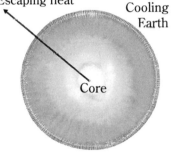

Escaping heat

Cooling Earth

Core

Another problem with Darwin's time-scale was that the interior of the Earth is still hot, as proved by volcanic eruptions. However, the English physicist William Thomson calculated that our planet should have cooled down in only about 20 million years, even if it was molten at the beginning.

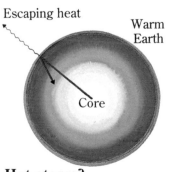

Escaping heat

Warm Earth

Core

Hot atoms?

The answers to the problems of timing

The nucleus of a uranium atom contains 238 nuclear particles. Over billions of years 32 of these are lost, leaving a lead atom which contains 206 particles

(above) lay in the tiniest objects of all – *atoms*. The atoms of *radioactive* elements such as uranium are slowly changing, giving out heat energy as they do so, and these atoms are found in the Earth's rocks, forming a permanent warm layer. The Sun has been shining for thousands of millions of years using the energy given out when one kind of atom changes into another.

Moon rock

Radioactive atoms can also be used as clocks. Over thousands of millions of years, atoms of uranium change into atoms of lead. By measuring the amount of lead that has been produced, physicists learn how long ago the rock containing the uranium was formed. Moon rocks brought back from the Apollo landings have been dated in this way, and some are over 4 billion years old.

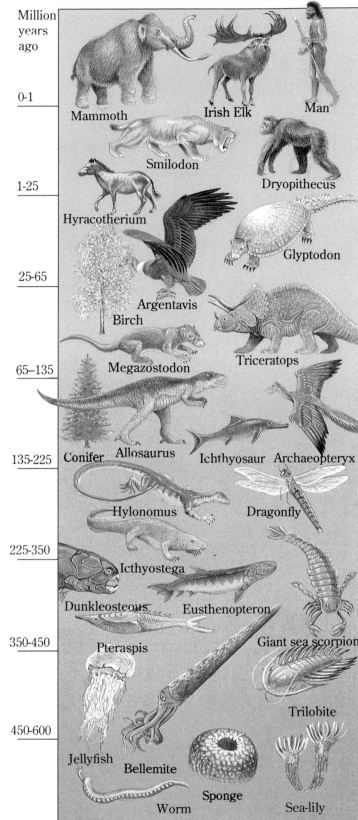

Million years ago

0-1

Mammoth   Irish Elk   Man

Smilodon

Dryopithecus

Hyracotherium

1-25

Birch

Glyptodon

25-65

Argentavis

Triceratops

65–135

Megazostodon

135-225

Conifer   Allosaurus   Ichthyosaur   Archaeopteryx

Hylonomus

Dragonfly

225-350

Icthyostega

Dunkleosteous   Eusthenopteron

350-450

Pteraspis

Giant sea scorpion

Trilobite

450-600

Jellyfish

Bellemite

Sponge

Sea-lily

Worm

Ages of Earth

This chart shows some of the more important plants and animals that have evolved during the past 600 million years. The earliest creatures lived in the sea. The dinosaurs died out suddenly, about 65 million years ago, perhaps because the Earth collided with another body (see page 19).

How the solar system began?

The lower illustration shows Ptolemy's Earth-centred system. The Sun orbits the Earth between the paths of Venus and Mars. The right hand illustration shows the correct sun-centred system

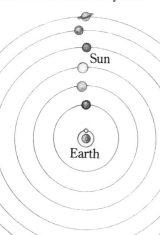

Earth

Sun

Earth

Sun

Ptolemy's Earth-centred Universe (AD 150) was accepted as correct for about 1500 years. Astronomers also believed that the Earth and heavenly bodies just came into existence.

Copernicus, in 1543, suggested that the Sun is at the centre of the Universe, with the planets and stars turning around it. This meant that the other planets might be worlds like the Earth.

Once astronomers realised that the solar system consists of a family of planets orbiting the Sun, it was natural to wonder how it was formed. The Sun is a shining star, while the planets are much smaller, shining in the sky by the Sun's reflected light. Why are such different bodies found together?

Some early theories suggested that the planets formed out of material pulled out of the Sun by a passing star. Since stars are normally very far apart, this meant that the formation of the solar system was an unlikely accident.

Other solar systems
By the 1920s, astronomers had evidence that other stars also have planets orbiting around them. Therefore they had to look for a much more likely way in which planets could be formed. Better theories of how stars themselves formed showed that planets could be built up from a cloud of gas and tiny particles – a *nebula* – at the same time as the star.

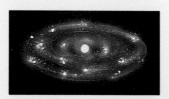

How the solar system formed?

1. The Sun began to form about 4 billion years ago, as one of a cluster of stars inside a dark nebula. It was spinning very rapidly, surrounded by a huge rotating ring of gas and dust. Most of this was hydrogen.

2. The solid particles inside the ring began to strike each other and stick together. The larger they grew, the stronger their gravity became. Smaller bodies were attracted to nearby larger ones, and gas atoms began to form cloudy atmospheres around them.

3. At one point there were a few large bodies and still billions of much smaller ones. Many of these were swung far off into space by the gravitational force of the larger bodies. These became comets (see pages 24–25), following huge orbits that go far beyond the outer planets.

4. Other small bodies kept hitting each other and breaking up again, forming the minor planets (page 15). Others became moons or satellites of the larger planets. A few hundred million years after its formation, the solar system more or less resembled its present form.

Another solar system?
More than 150 stars have been discovered with clouds of particles around them, as the Sun must have done when the planets were being formed. The star Beta Pictoris is one of these, and this is how it might appear if viewed from close up. Planets may already have formed in this cloud.

Mars

Venus

Sun

Earth

Mercury

Jupiter

Saturn

Uranus

Neptune

Pluto

5. By about 3 billion years ago, the collisions were dying down. The planets' gravity had pulled their orbits into line with each other, and the remaining gas and fine dust had been lost into space. On the Earth, the first living things were forming.

What the nearer planets are like?

Once telescopes were invented in 1608, astronomers began to peer across space at the planets. Innermost Mercury was too tiny to see at all clearly. Venus appeared to be covered with cloud, while Mars had bright polar caps and dark markings. Some people thought that Venus and Mars might even be inhabited by living beings.

However, despite patient observation over centuries, astronomers learned far more about these planets when they sent out space probes to photograph and study them.

Mercury
Mercury has a heavily cratered surface. A mountain-ringed plain 1300 kilometres across, called the Caloris Basin, was caused by a rocky body slamming into Mercury about 4 billion years ago.

Caloris basin

Mercury

Venus

Venus
Venus is cloaked inside a thick atmosphere, but radio waves can pass through it. The first crude maps were made by radar, bouncing radio waves off its surface. The Magellan orbiter (below) has now mapped almost the whole surface in minute detail by this method. The atmosphere traps the Sun's heat, and the surface temperature is about 470°C. This is hot enough to bake clay pots.

Every 3½ hours, as it passed close to Venus, Magellan observed a strip of the planet. During the rest of its orbit, the spacecraft radioed the information back to Earth

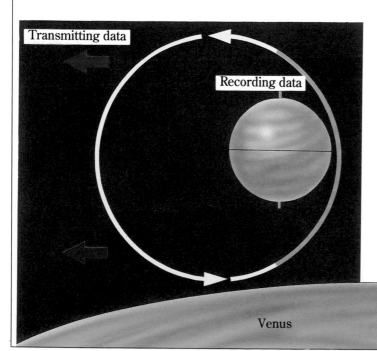

Transmitting data

Recording data

Venus

14

Mars

Early this century, many people thought there might be life on Mars. The American astronomer Percival Lowell believed that its inhabitants had built canals on Earth to bring water from the polar caps to the deserts. Unfortunately Mars is too far away from the Earth to be seen in great detail, and space probes have shown that it is a desert world with craters and huge ravines. The most spectacular space mission to Mars was in 1976, when two Viking probes landed *modules* on the surface. These found a chill surface always below 0°C, a thin carbon dioxide atmosphere, and a sky made pink by airborne dust. They did not find any sign of life.

Sun

Venus

Mercury

Earth

Mars

Asteroid belt

Ceres

Asteroids

Beyond Mars, in the wide gap before Jupiter, orbit the minor planets or asteroids. They seem to be the remains of some very small planets that formed at the birth of the solar system, collided with each other, and broke up again.

Viking probe

Vesta

Pallas

Juno

A view of the dusty, rock strewn surface of Mars, taken by one of the two Viking probes, with part of the spacecraft visible in the foreground

What the outer planets are like?

In January 1610, the Italian *philosopher* Galileo Galilei pointed his small home-made telescope towards Jupiter. He was surprised to see some faint star-like objects very near it, and realised that they were orbiting the planet like moons. This was a very important discovery. Ptolemy's Earth-centred Universe was still widely accepted, but Galileo had discovered that not everything in the Universe revolves around the Earth.

Astronomers soon realised that Jupiter is far larger than the Earth. So are the other giant planets Saturn, Uranus and Neptune. They are not at all like the inner planets because their globes are made mostly of liquid hydrogen. Saturn is the outermost planet easily visible with the naked eye. Uranus, Neptune and Pluto were discovered using telescopes.

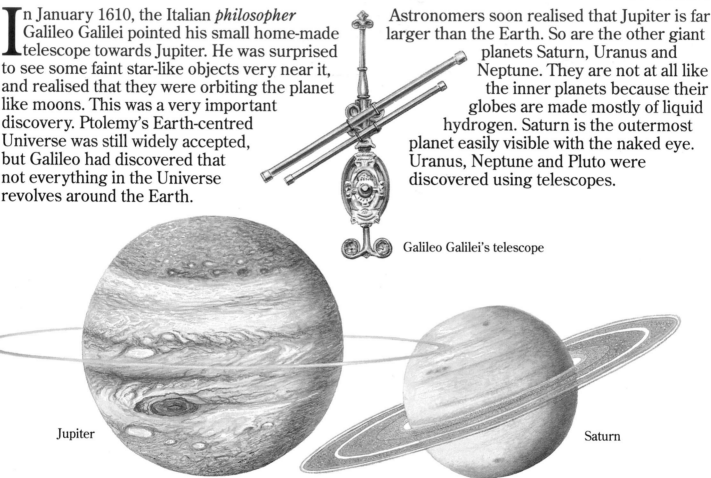

Galileo Galilei's telescope

Jupiter

Saturn

Jupiter photographed by Voyager 1 in 1979. Two satellites are visible: the right hand one is in front of the Great Red Spot

Jupiter

Jupiter is ten times the Earth's diameter, and even the primitive 17th century telescopes allowed observers to see cloud markings on its surface. These showed that its huge bulk spins once in less than ten hours – the shortest 'day' of all the planets. Pioneer and Voyager space probes obtained the first detailed views of its many *satellites* (left).

Saturn

Saturn was also observed by Galileo. He thought it was a triple planet. But the two smaller 'planets' on either side of Saturn were seen by the Dutch observer Christiaan Huygens to be part of a flat ring surrounding the planet. Saturn is a smaller planet than Jupiter, but one of its moons, Titan, is the largest satellite in the solar system.

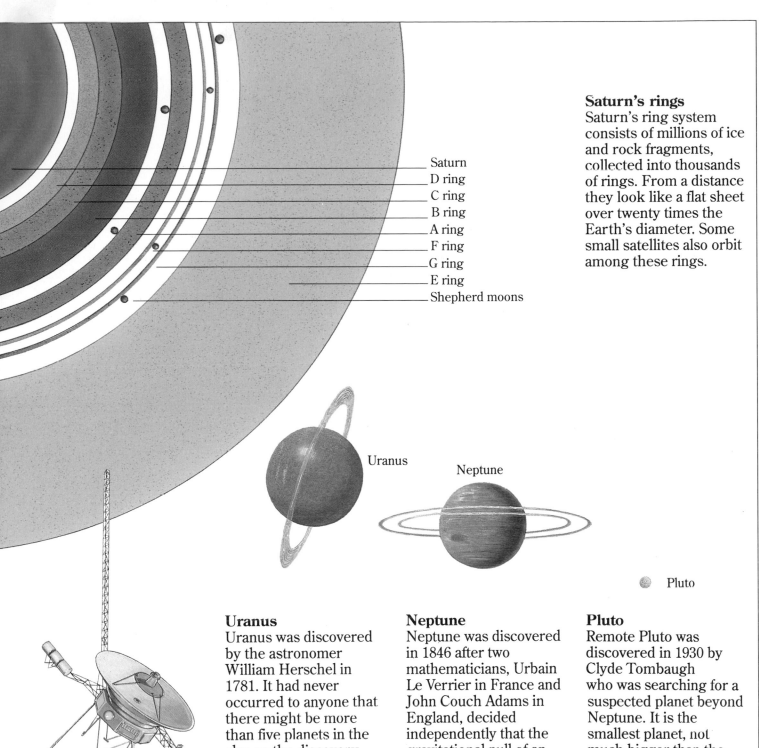

Saturn
D ring
C ring
B ring
A ring
F ring
G ring
E ring
Shepherd moons

Uranus

Neptune

Pluto

Saturn's rings

Saturn's ring system consists of millions of ice and rock fragments, collected into thousands of rings. From a distance they look like a flat sheet over twenty times the Earth's diameter. Some small satellites also orbit among these rings.

Space probe

Voyager 2 is the most successful space probe ever launched. Between 1977 and 1989 it passed all four giant planets, and transmitted thousands of images of each one. It is now heading towards the stars, but is expected to keep sending back signals until about 2020.

Uranus

Uranus was discovered by the astronomer William Herschel in 1781. It had never occurred to anyone that there might be more than five planets in the sky, so the discovery came as a complete surprise. Another surprise was the detection in 1977 of nine very narrow rings around the planet. When Voyager 2 passed Uranus in 1986 it discovered more rings, as well as ten very small satellites in addition to the five previously known.

Neptune

Neptune was discovered in 1846 after two mathematicians, Urbain Le Verrier in France and John Couch Adams in England, decided independently that the gravitational pull of an unknown planet was pulling on Uranus and calculated where it must be. Almost nothing was known about Neptune until Voyager 2 passed it in 1989. It has very faint rings, and winds blow through its bitterly cold cloud layers at up to 2000 km/h.

Pluto

Remote Pluto was discovered in 1930 by Clyde Tombaugh who was searching for a suspected planet beyond Neptune. It is the smallest planet, not much bigger than the Moon. Pluto's satellite Charon is half its own diameter, so that the two bodies almost form a small double planet. It takes 248 years to orbit the Sun, and for 20 of these (between 1979 and 1999) it is closer to the Sun than Neptune, which is currently the outermost planet.

Why there are craters on the Moon?

The lunar craters are unlike anything visible on the Earth's surface. Some are far bigger than the largest cities and their suburbs. A popular idea in Victorian times was the 'fiery fountain' theory. They thought that a volcanic vent spouted material into a raised ring, producing a circular wall with a volcanic mountain at the centre.

At that time, astronomers had not observed craters on any other planets or satellites, and so they thought that the Moon's surface was special. Now that space probes have shown large and small craters on almost every rocky surface in the solar system, the Moon is seen to be normal. The craters are the result of impacts with smaller space bodies, and most occurred more than 3 billion years ago.

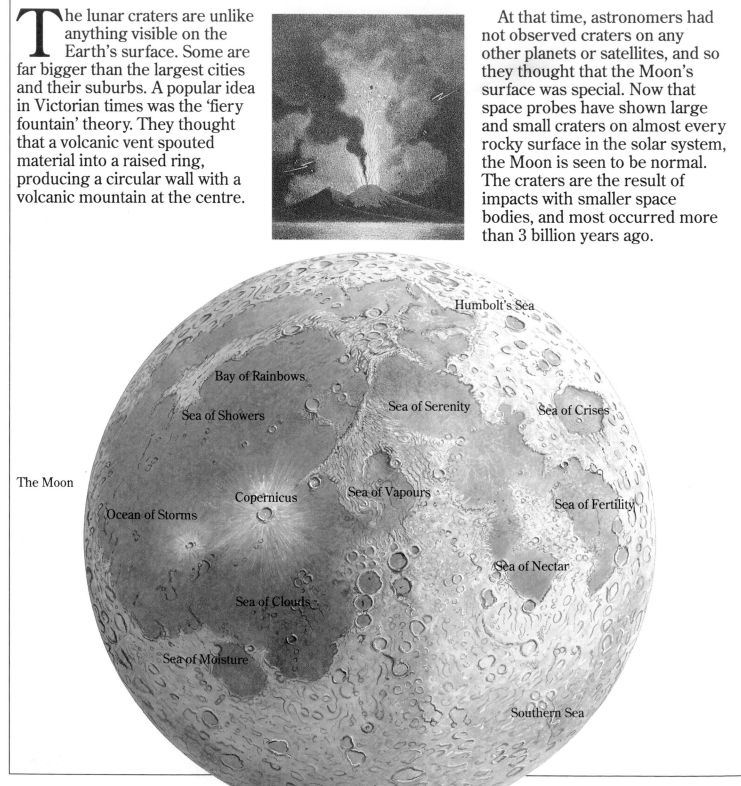

Humbolt's Sea

Bay of Rainbows

Sea of Serenity

Sea of Crises

Sea of Showers

The Moon

Copernicus

Sea of Vapours

Sea of Fertility

Ocean of Storms

Sea of Nectar

Sea of Clouds

Sea of Moisture

Southern Sea

Earth's craters

There were once craters on the Earth, but they have been worn away by wind and water, as well as the movements of the crust. A rare exception, Meteor Crater in

Arizona, is 1 km across and was formed by an impact with a body about 30 metres across moving at about 30 km/s between 25,000 and 50,000 years ago.

Aerial view of Meteor Crater in Arizona

Impact

In a meteorite impact, the meteor is immediately turned to *vapour* by the tremendous energy released. Shock waves travel deep and wide into the surrounding crust, and the punched-down surface may rebound to form a central hill or even mountain, as seen in many of the largest lunar craters. The diameter of the crater will be twenty or more times the diameter of the body causing it.

Wipe out

The chances of the Earth or Moon suffering a devastating collision with an object 10-kilometres wide are now put at about one every 100 million years. It is possible that a tremendous impact 65 million years ago in Central America caused the Earth's surface to be darkened and chilled under a black cloud of dust that lasted for several years. The dark and cold could have killed off many plants and the animals – including dinosaurs – that fed on them.

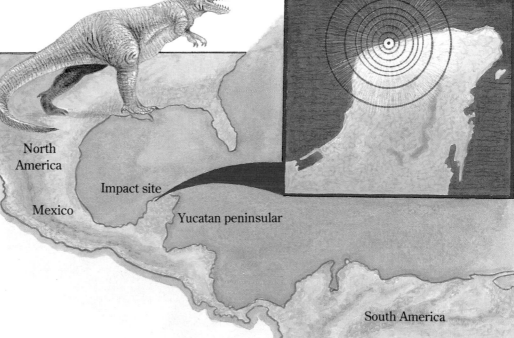

North America

Mexico

Impact site

Yucatan peninsular

South America

Why the Moon shows phases?

The month was originally the period of time the Moon took to pass through its phases. The Moon's phase was an important factor in agricultural communities before powerful artificial light became available, and some cultures still use a lunar month in their calendar.

Even early astronomers understood quite well why the Moon passes through phases. This was because they realised that the Sun lights up the Moon, and the Moon revolves around the Earth. Only half of the Moon is lit up by the Sun at any one time. As it orbits the Earth, our view of this half keeps changing, and so the phase changes from a thin crescent to a complete round disc.

Sometimes the Moon passes in front of the Sun, causing a solar eclipse. At other times it passes through the Earth's shadow, producing a lunar eclipse.

The phases
The Moon keeps the same face turned permanently towards the Earth. As the phase changes, we see different surface features come into the sunlight and then disappear again about two weeks later.

Last quarter

A full circle
The lunar month – the time it takes the Moon to return to the same phase – is about 29 days 12 hours long.

New Moon

Full Moon

First quarter

First Quarter
One week after New Moon it appears as a perfect half. This is called the First Quarter, because it has covered one quarter of its monthly orbit.

Evening crescent
Soon after New Moon the moon appears in the evening sky as a narrow crescent.

Full Moon
In another week the moon is full. The Full Moon is opposite the Sun in the sky.

Last Quarter
Three weeks after New Moon it is at the Third or Last Quarter.

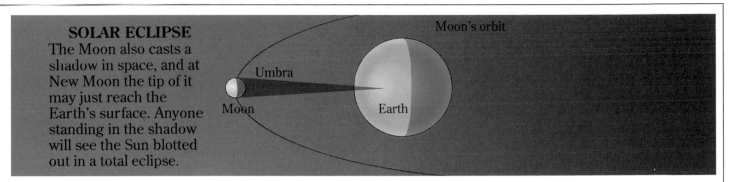

SOLAR ECLIPSE

The Moon also casts a shadow in space, and at New Moon the tip of it may just reach the Earth's surface. Anyone standing in the shadow will see the Sun blotted out in a total eclipse.

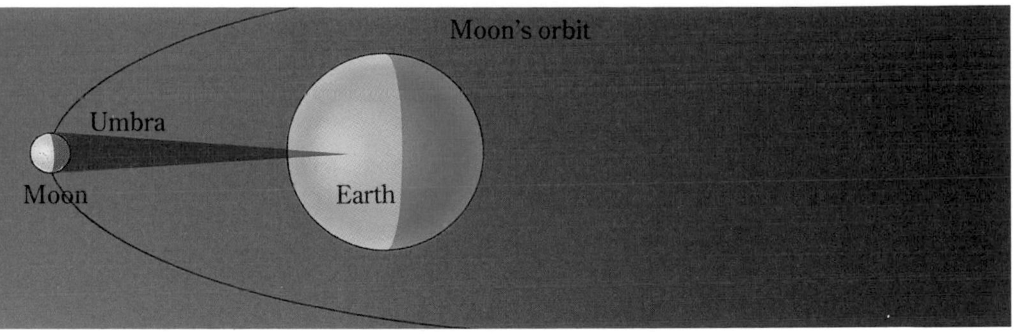

Spring tides

Newton's theory of gravity showed why the Moon controls the tides. Its gravitational force pulls the oceans into a bulge a few metres high, which remains pointing near the Moon as the Earth spins inside it. The far-off Sun has a weaker pull.

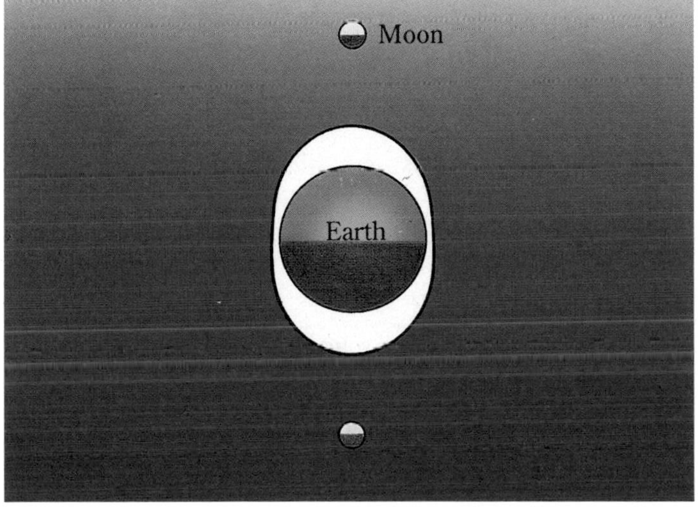

Neap tides

Not all high tides are the same. Strong spring tides occur when the Moon and Sun are pulling in the same line, at New or Full Moon. Weak neap tides occur when the Sun and Moon are pulling across each other, at First or Last Quarter.

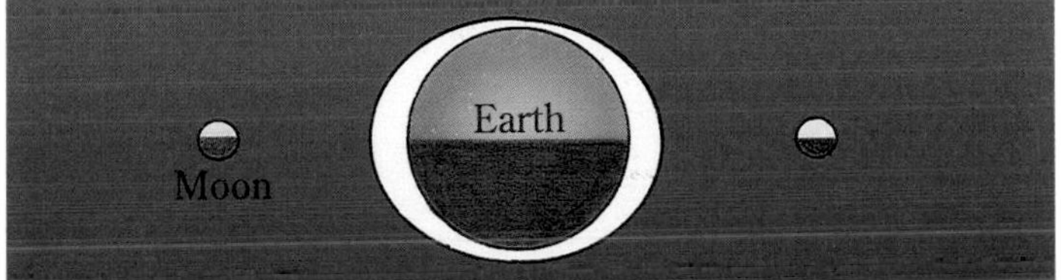

Dawn crescent

Two or three days before the next New Moon, it is visible as a thin crescent in the dawn sky.

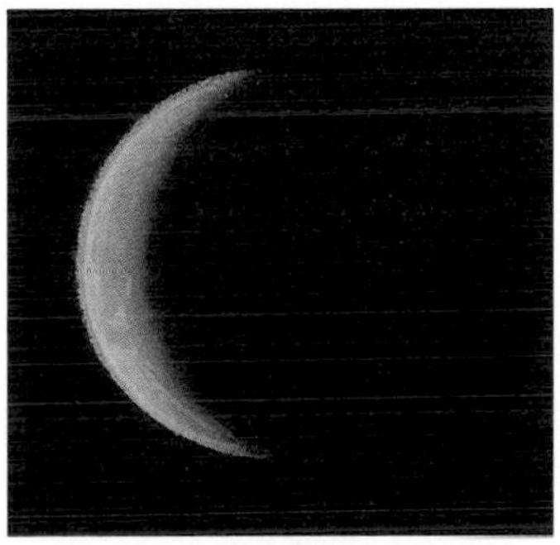

Copper moon

When the Moon is full, it sometimes passes into the Earth's shadow. It usually turns a dull copper colour because red light passes through our atmosphere into the shadow.

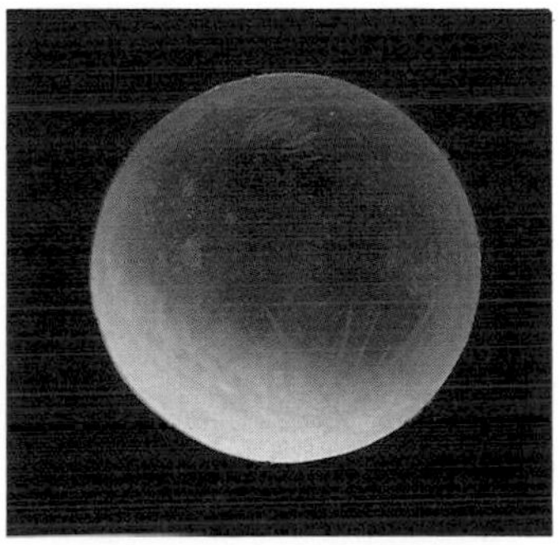

Slowing down

The ocean bulge is gradually slowing down the Moon, which is very slowly spiralling away from the Earth. Eventually it will appear only 2/3 as wide as it does now, taking 55 days to orbit the Earth once.

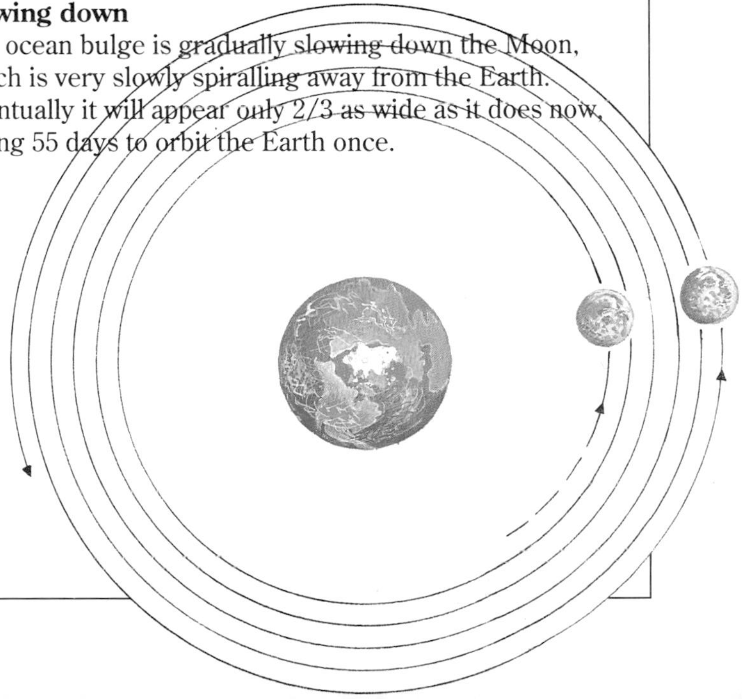

What sunspots are?

Chinese naked-eye records from about 2000 BC mention spots on the Sun. However, it is extremely dangerous to look at or near the Sun at any time, even when it is a dull red colour. Its invisible *rays* can damage the eye permanently even when it looks dim.

Old beliefs about the Sun sound strange to our ears. In the 19th century it was thought that sunspots might be holes in a shining layer, revealing its dark interior.

In the mid-19th century a German amateur astronomer, Hofrath Schwabe, observed the Sun on every possible day for about 30 years and discovered that sunspots are more frequent every 11 years or so. This is known as the solar cycle.

By the beginning of this century scientists realised that sunspots are cooler areas of the Sun's bright surface (but still very hot – about 4,000°C compared with 5,500°C). They occur where gigantic *magnetic fields* arc through the Sun's bright surface. These cool the surface, making it darker. Small sunspots last for a few days. Large ones may last for months.

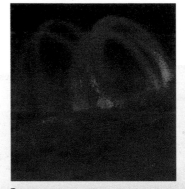 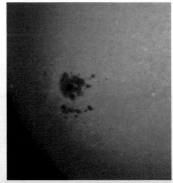

Loops
Prominences are loops of hydrogen. They flow along magnetic arcs that break through the Sun's surface.

Centres of sunspots
The dark centre of a sunspot is called the umbra. The lighter area around it is called the penumbra.

The size of sunspots
The Sun is 100 times the diameter of the Earth, so even a very small sunspot will be wider than our planet's diameter. A prominence like this one could completely swallow up the Earth, and some are far larger.

Earth

AURORA

Atomic particles, especially protons (part of an atom's nucleus) and electrons (which go round the nucleus), pour out from the Sun at about 450 km/s. These form the solar wind. Magnetic eruptions at the Sun's surface can produce extra bursts of particles which are caught by the Earth's magnetic field. These particles follow the lines of magnetic force that curve down over the North and South Poles, and strike atoms of oxygen, nitrogen and other *elements* high in the atmosphere. When this happens the atoms glow, causing an aurora.

These night-time displays are most frequent when the solar cycle is at maximum activity, and they are most likely to be seen by observers in places fairly near the Earth's poles, such as northern Europe and Canada.

| 1880 | 1890 | 1900 | 1910 | 1920 | 1930 | 1940 | 1950 | 1960 | 1970 |

Solar activity
This chart shows how the area of the Sun covered by sunspots has changed over a period of 100 years. Every 11 years or so, when the solar cycle is at a maximum, sunspots are most numerous. Some solar cycles are more active than others, the maximum in 1958 being particularly strong.

The weather
Does the Sun influence the weather? There is some evidence that it does. For example, between 1645 and 1715 there seem to have been very few sunspots, and the weather in Europe, for example, was exceptionally cold.

Where comets come from?

For thousands of years, comets were seen as frightening signs, foretelling disaster, until Edmund Halley proved that they are members of the solar system. Most are very small icy objects packed with black rocky dust, just a few kilometres across. In the early days of the solar system they passed near one of the larger planets – probably Jupiter – and its gravity speeded them up so much that they were almost flung out of the solar system altogether.

This is how a bright comet appears in an old drawing, made when comets were thought to foretell disaster

They then found themselves moving along enormous orbits that took them far beyond Pluto before they swung back towards the Sun. It has been estimated that there could be two billion comets in a region of space far beyond Pluto.

Every now and then the gravitational attraction of one comet passing another changes the comet's path and it heads towards the Sun, perhaps taking ten thousand years to do so. As it whirls round the Sun the heat turns the powdery rock and ice to gas and dust. In the vacuum of space this cloud expands to fill a huge volume very thinly, and the solar wind brushes the cloud back to form a tail.

Virgo

Sun

Earth

Halley's comet
The nucleus of Halley's Comet is only about 2 km across. In 1986 the dust and gas from this extended for about 100,000,000 km.

A comet's orbit
At its closest to the Sun, Halley's Comet is nearer than Venus. Some comets pass closer than Mercury, or may even collide with the Sun. A few unusual comets have almost circular orbits, more like planets.

Tycho's comet

The brilliant comet of 1577, celebrated on this coin, was particularly important because the astronomer Tycho Brahe observed it carefully with his elaborate naked-eye sighting instruments. He realised that it was not something in the Earth's atmosphere, as many people believed, but was passing through space beyond the Moon.

Ancient sightings

Halley's Comet happened to pass near the Earth and Sun in 1066, at the time of the Battle of Hastings in England. This scene from the Bayeux Tapestry shows the English King Harold realising that the comet's appearance may foretell defeat at the hands of the Norman king William the Conqueror.

Comets are named after the person or people who discover them. This photograph shows Comet Brorsen-Metcalf on September 4, 1989.

EDMUND HALLEY

Edmund Halley (1656–1742) was a remarkable man. At the age of 20 he sailed to the southern hemisphere to make the first catalogue of stars invisible from Europe, and in 1699 he voyaged to the Antarctic to study the Earth's magnetic field. It was thanks to his money that Newton's theory of gravitation was published in 1687, and in 1720 he became Astronomer Royal!

In 1705 he published the results of his researches into comets observed in 1456, 1531, 1607 and 1682. He concluded that they were the same body travelling in a very elongated orbit that took it far from the Sun and Earth and back again in a period of about 76 years. Halley predicted that it would return again in 1758, which it did, although by this time he was dead. He had proved beyond all doubt that this particular comet, at least, is a member of the solar system.

What stars are made of?

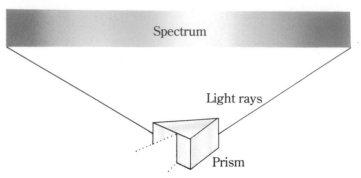

Until the middle of the 19th century astronomers did not even think of trying to find out what the stars are made of, because there seemed to be no way of ever finding out.

This all changed when a German physicist called Gustav Robert Kirchoff experimented with light passing through a prism. He discovered that the pattern of dark lines in the *spectrum* was different according to the elements in the substance giving out the light.

This was a tremendous breakthrough. By examining the spectrum of a star, no matter how far away it is, astronomers can see what elements are in it.

THE SPECTRUM
White light is the effect made on the eye by light of all the colours of the rainbow combined together. To see the separate colours, white light is passed through a prism, producing a spectrum.

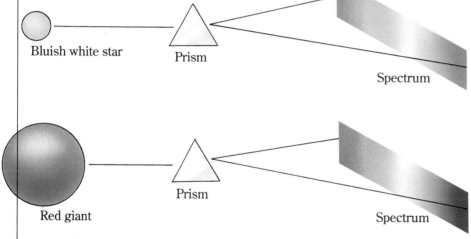

Comparing spectra
Very hot stars are white or bluish. They produce a fairly even spectrum of colours, crossed by dark lines. These lines in the spectrum are produced by different elements in the star, such as hydrogen, sodium and calcium. Cool stars are much redder, so the red end of the spectrum is stronger than the violet end. A cool star could be a red giant or a red dwarf.

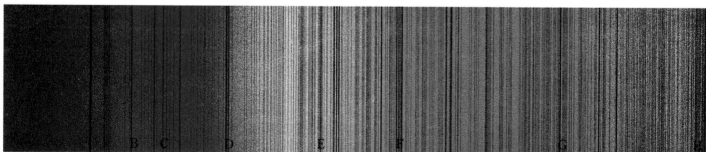

The Sun's spectrum
This is what the spectrum of the Sun looks like. Altogether it contains thousands of dark lines. The picture indicates the elements causing some of the lines.

B Oxygen
C Hydrogen
D Sodium
E Iron
F Hydrogen
G Iron and calcium
H Calcium

Stars in general
Most stars are very similar as far as the elements in them are concerned. They contain about 90% hydrogen, 9% helium, and 1% of the other 90 elements that occur in the Universe. What makes them different is their size, temperature and brightness.

Main sequence stars

Ordinary stars like the Sun are very common. They belong to a family called the main sequence. Main sequence stars are rather like people between about 18 and 50 in a human population – they are passing through their years of prime health and strength. The brightest main sequence stars are about a thousand times as bright as the Sun, and the dimmest are about one thousandth as bright. In colour they range from bluish-white to yellow, and most of the stars visible in the night sky are of this kind. Most keep shining for thousands of millions of years, and some may have planets orbiting around them.

Most keep shining for billions of years, and some may have planets orbiting around them.

Blue giants

Blue giants, which are the hottest stars, are rare. Their surface temperature is about 20,000 C – four times as hot as the Sun – and they shine about 10,000 times as brightly. However, blue giants do not last long – in just a few million years they have used up most of their hydrogen fuel, and may collapse in a violent shock that blows the whole star apart as a *supernova*.

Giants

Red giants and supergiants are the largest stars – they could be larger than the Earth's orbit around the Sun. A main sequence star turns into a red giant towards the end of its life, puffing its outer layers of hydrogen into space as an enormous glowing cloud. Finally, a red giant collapses into a tiny white dwarf.

Red dwarfs

Red dwarf stars are much smaller than the Sun, although still much larger than planets. As a rule, the more material (mass) a star has, the brighter it shines. Red dwarfs have very low masses and give out less than one ten-thousandth of the Sun's light. At a temperature of only 3000°C, their surfaces are even cooler than the centre of a sunspot. There are probably more red dwarfs in the Universe than any other kind of star.

White dwarfs

A white dwarf star is the Earth-sized remains of an old star. A teaspoonful of its material would weigh several tonnes, but neutron stars (page 31) are much denser than this. The Sun will one day become a white dwarf.

The distance to the stars?

Background stars

61 Cygni

June Sun Earth January

Before the 17th century, most people thought that the stars really were fixed to the inside of a huge, invisible sphere with the Earth at the centre, turning once a day. One estimate as to their distance from the Earth was about 80,000,000 km. This is only half the true distance to the Sun!

When telescopes brought fainter and fainter stars into view, astronomers became convinced that they really were looking into remote space. The problem of measuring the distance to the stars became extremely important.

However, the first successful measurement was not made until 1838, when the German astronomer Friedrich Bessel used a method based on *parallax*.

A plan of the Universe as imagined by the astronomer Tycho Brahe around 1580. He thought that the stars were dim objects not much further away than the planets.

Parallax theory
Bessel very carefully measured the angles between his target star, known as 61 Cygni, and other stars that he thought were much further away.

Six months later, he measured these angles again. During this time the Earth had moved to the other side of its orbit around the Sun, a distance of about 300,000,000 km. This caused a shift in the angles as 61 Cygni appeared to move from side to side in front of the more distant stars.

The shift measured by Bessel was very small – about the same as the thickness of a human hair viewed from 150 metres. Calculations showed that 61 Cygni must be about 100,000 billion kilometres away from the Sun.

A distant star appears fainter than a nearby one of the same true brightness or luminosity. You can see the effect for yourself by looking down a street at a line of identical street lamps.

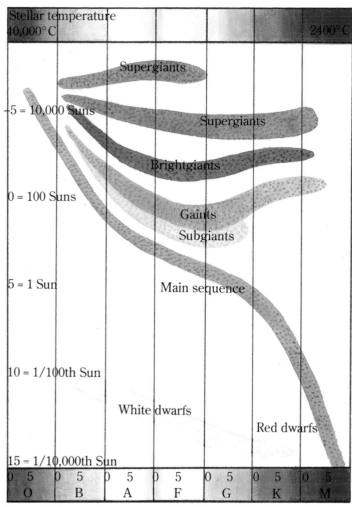

Stellar temperature
40,000°C   2400°C

Supergiants

-5 = 10,000 Suns

Supergiants

Brightgiants

0 = 100 Suns

Giants

Subgiants

5 = 1 Sun   Main sequence

10 = 1/100th Sun

White dwarfs

Red dwarfs

15 = 1/10,000th Sun

0 5	0 5	0 5	0 5	0 5	0 5	0 5
O	B	A	F	G	K	M

Spectral class

Misleading brightness

The brightness of the stars as they appear in the sky is misleading. If one star is nearer to the Sun than a similar one, it will appear brighter. For example, the stars Rigel and Mintaka in the constellation Orion are of similar luminosity (about 40,000 times the brightness of the Sun), but Rigel is about twice as close to us, and appears much brighter. Betelgeuse is less luminous than Rigel, but appears about as bright because it is closer.

Hertzsprung and Russell

Most stars are too far away to show any parallax at all, so how can their distances be measured? A breakthrough came in 1913 when two astronomers, Ejnar Hertzsprung and Henry Norris Russell, independently discovered that the true brightness or *luminosity* of most stars depends upon their colour, which is fairly easy to assess.

The hottest (bluest) stars are also the most luminous; the coolest (reddest) stars are the dimmest. This is shown on the famous Hertzsprung-Russell Diagram.

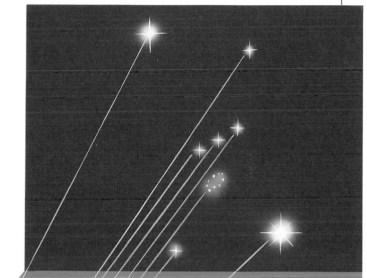
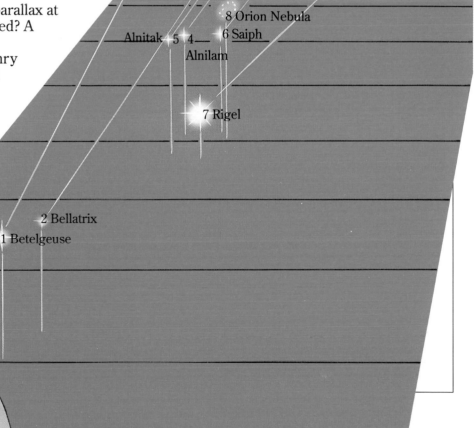

3 Mintaka

8 Orion Nebula

6 Saiph

Alnitak 5 4

Alnilam

7 Rigel

2 Bellatrix

1 Betelgeuse

What a black hole is?

No one has ever seen a black hole. In fact, a black hole is invisible. But two completely separate pieces of research came together to expose them.

Firstly, one of Einstein's predictions in his Special Relativity theory of 1907 was that space curves very slightly near objects with strong gravity, such as the Sun. Although space is invisible, it controls the passage of a light-ray through it, which can be used as a marker. Secondly, in the 1930s, physicists realised that dying stars might collapse upon themselves and shrink down to the size of a small asteroid. They would be *neutron stars*, made up of the solid matter found in an atomic nucleus.

Formation of a black hole

The gravity around a neutron star could be so intense that space would be curved back on itself. Light from the star could not escape. The star would become an invisible black hole.

Curving space

Space-bending was proved by a famous experiment at the solar eclipse of 1919. The sky became dark enough for stars to be photographed near the Sun, and then compared with their normal position.

Their light curved slightly as it passed near the Sun's powerful gravity. This made them appear to be in a slightly different position in the sky.

Are neutron stars possible?

In 1932 two American astronomers, Walter Baade and Fritz Zwicky, predicted that neutron stars could be produced when a star dies.

A star is like a continuously-exploding atomic bomb. It does not blow up because gravity holds it together. When its *atomic reactor* begins to run out of fuel it may suddenly collapse.

An ordinary star like the Sun will not produce a neutron star. Baade and Zwicky were thinking of a very massive star, with as much material as about fifty of our Suns. If this collapsed, the atoms near its centre would be squashed into a neutron star just a few kilometres across, but containing as much material as several stars like the Sun!

Discovering a black hole

A black hole is invisible, but astronomers think they have discovered some by their pull of gravity on a nearby visible star, or by

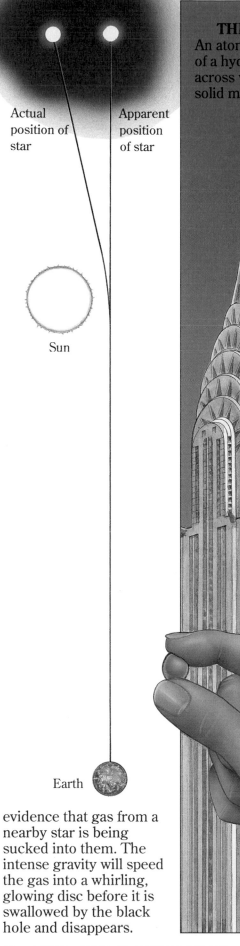

Actual position of star

Apparent position of star

Sun

Earth

evidence that gas from a nearby star is being sucked into them. The intense gravity will speed the gas into a whirling, glowing disc before it is swallowed by the black hole and disappears.

THE DENSITY OF A NEUTRON STAR

An atom is almost all empty space. A model of a hydrogen atom measuring 50 metres across would contain only a pinhead amount of solid material.

Hydrogen is the most common element in a star, and when its atoms are crushed inside a neutron star so that the solid remains, or neutrons, are pressed together, its density becomes enormously high. A pea-sized piece of a neutron star would weigh as much as a street of office blocks.

Who invented the constellations?

Constellations are patterns of stars named after mythical people, animals, or even quite ordinary objects. The origin of many of the constellation names is lost in history.

The star catalogue of Ptolemy (AD 150) contained 48 constellations known in his time, such as the Great Bear (Ursa Major), Orion, and other well-known groups.

In the 16th century, when explorers from Europe reached the southern hemisphere and saw stars invisible from their homelands, new constellations had to be 'invented'. Some seem quite modern, such as the Air Pump (Antlia), the Clock (Horologium), and

the Microscope (Microscopium), all introduced by the French astronomer Nicolas Louis de Lacaille in 1763.

This map, dated 1650, shows the constellations of the northern sky (left) and the southern sky (right). Some extra constellations were added to the southern sky after this date

The Zodiac
The oldest constellations are probably the 12 constellations of the Zodiac. The Zodiac is the band of sky around which the Sun, Moon and planets appear to move. This is because it lies in the same plane as the Earth and other planets move.

The Sun appears to move around the Zodiac once a year because of the Earth's movement along its orbit. During this time it spends about one month passing through each constellation, although at that time the stars

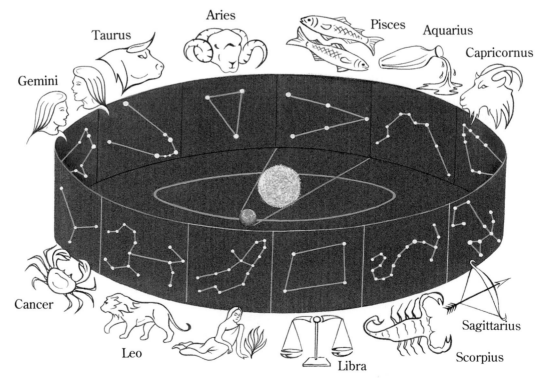

themselves are not visible because it lies in the daylight sky. Six months later, the constellation is in the

midnight sky. Babylonian astronomers named the 12 Zodiacal constellations about 5000 years ago.

Libra, the Scales
The sun passes through this Zodiacal constellation between about October 31 and November 22 every year.

Northern hemisphere constellations

1 Equuleus, the little horse
2 Delphinus, the dolphin
3 Pegasus
4 Pisces, the fishes
5 Cetus, the sea monster
6 Aries, the ram
7 Triangulum, the triangle
8 Andromeda
9 Lacerta, the lizard
10 Cygnus, the swan
11 Sagitta, the arrow
12 Aquila, the eagle
13 Lyra, the lyre
14 Cepheus
15 Cassiopeia
16 Perseus
17 Camelopardalis, the giraffe
18 Auriga, the charioteer
19 Taurus, the bull
20 Orion
21 Lynx
22 Polaris, the pole star
23 Ursa Minor, the little bear
24 Draco, the dragon
25 Hercules
26 Ophiuchus, the serpent bearer
27 Serpens, the serpent
28 Corona Borealis, the northern crown
29 Bootes, the herdsman
30 Ursa Major, the great bear
31 Gemini, the twins
32 Cancer, the crab
33 Canis Minor, the little dog
34 Hydra, the water snake
35 Leo, the lion
36 Leo minor, the little lion
37 Canes Venatici, the hunting dogs
38 Coma Berenices, Berenices' hair
39 Virgo, the virgin
40 Vulpecula, the fox

Southern hemisphere constellations

1 Cetus, the whale
2 Sculptor
3 Aquarius, the water bearer
4 Piscis Austrinus, the southern fish
5 Capricornus, the sea-goat
6 Grus, the crane
7 Phoenix
8 Fornax, the furnace
9 Eridanus, River Eridanus

Northern hemisphere

Southern hemisphere

10 Hydrus, the lesser water snake
11 Tucana, the toucan
12 Indus, the Indian
13 Sagittarius, the archer
14 Aquila, the eagle
15 Corona Australis,
  the southern crown
16 Pavo, the peacock
17 Octans, the octant
18 Dorado, the swordfish
19 Pictor, the painter
20 Columba, the dove
21 Lepus, the hare
22 Orion, the hunter
23 Monoceros, the unicorn
24 Canis Major, the great dog
25 Puppis, the poop of Argo
26 Carina, the keel of Argo
27 Volans, the flying fish
28 Chamæleon, the chameleon
29 Apus, the bird of paradise

30 Triangulum Australe
  the southern triangle
31 Ara, the altar
32 Scorpius, the scorpion
33 Serpens, the serpent
34 Ophiuchus, the serpent bearer
35 Lupus, the wolf
36 Centaurus, the centaur
37 Crux, the southern cross
38 Musca, the fly
39 Vela, the sails of Argo
40 Pyxis, the mariner's compass
41 Hydra, the water snake
42 Sextans, the sextant
43 Crater, the cup
44 Corvus, the crow
45 Libra, the scales
46 Virgo, the virgin
47 Reticulum, the net
48 Scutum, the shield
49 Telescopium, the telescope

How Do We Know

What the Milky Way is?

Before street lights began to lighten the night sky, even city-dwellers could see the stars in all their glory. Nowadays, the Milky Way can only be seen properly from dark country districts far from built-up areas.

Not surprisingly it was a source of wonder and mystery until Galileo and other early telescopic astronomers discovered that the Milky Way effect is caused by multitudes of faint stars, too dim to be seen separately with the naked eye.

But the reason why the stars were clustered together in a band remained a mystery. Then, in the late 19th century, astronomers discovered dim whirlpool-like objects in the sky which contained clouds of faint stars. Gradually they realised that the Milky Way effect could be explained if the Sun belonged to one of these spiral Milky Ways or galaxies.

We now know that the Milky Way galaxy contains spiral arms made up of stars, gas, and minute solid particles. It contains at least 100 billion stars, and as old stars die, new ones are born in the dark nebulae of the spiral arms.

Sun

Sun

Plan view of the Milky Way
The Milky Way galaxy measures about 100,000 light-years across. (A light-year is the distance a ray of light travels in one year: 9.5 million million kilometres.) Near the centre is a cloud of very old, red giant stars.

Side view
The arms are flattened, explaining our view of the 'Milky Way' effect when we look along them. The dust in the spiral arms forms a dark band. The rotating galaxy carries it around the centre once in 225 million years.

THE LOCAL GROUP

The Milky Way is not alone in space. It is the second-largest member of a cluster of about 30 galaxies in a cluster about two million light-years across, known as the Local Group.

Most of these galaxies are small, containing only a few million stars. The largest galaxy, also a spiral like the Milky Way, can be seen with the naked eye in the constellation of Andromeda, and has about four times as many stars as our own.

Andromeda

Our galaxy

Large Megellanic cloud

THE LARGE MAGELLANIC CLOUD

This galaxy is the nearest to us – about 160,000 light-years away – and was discovered from the south Atlantic by the explorer Ferdinand Magellan in 1520. In 1987 one of its stars exploded as a supernova, sending out more light than all the other stars put together.

What galaxies are?

Through a telescope, even the brightest galaxy looks like a faint, filmy smudge. In 1783 the Frenchman Charles Messier listed 39 galaxies without realising what they were.

In the 1850s the Earl of Rosse, in Ireland, studied one of these objects and discovered that it was spiral in shape. However, he thought that it was another solar system being formed among the Sun's neighbour stars.

But in the late 19th century photography was used to record much fainter details than the eye could see. These objects were at last discovered to be vast star systems far beyond our own Milky Way galaxy.

Millions of galaxies have now been recorded. Most of them are either spiral (like our own), elliptical, or irregular in shape. Supergiant galaxies may contain a million million stars – the smallest dwarf variety may contain only one million.

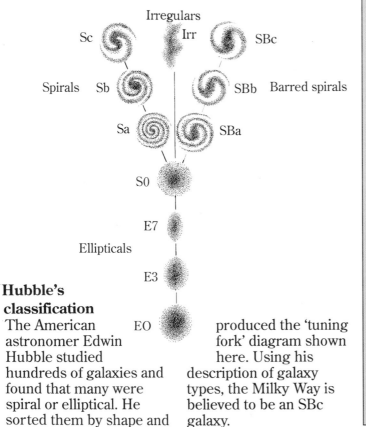

Hubble's classification

The American astronomer Edwin Hubble studied hundreds of galaxies and found that many were spiral or elliptical. He sorted them by shape and produced the 'tuning fork' diagram shown here. Using his description of galaxy types, the Milky Way is believed to be an SBc galaxy.

Herschel's greatest telescope was the largest in the world when built in 1789

WILLIAM HERSCHEL

William Herschel was born in Hanover, Germany, in 1738 and came to England as a musician. He became interested in astronomy, but could not afford to buy a telescope of his own. He taught himself to make lenses and mirrors and eventually built the largest telescope in the world (above) with a mirror 1.2 metres across.

He became famous when he discovered the planet Uranus in 1781, but his main interest was what he called 'the construction of the heavens'. He wondered if the stars of the Milky Way filled the entire Universe or if there were other galaxies of stars far away. He puzzled over the thousands of faint smudges of light revealed by his telescopes, but finally thought that they were simply clouds of luminous gas, or clusters of stars too distant to be resolved into points of light, belonging to our own star system. Most of these are now known to be remote galaxies.

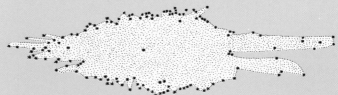

Star counts

Herschel counted the number of stars seen in his telescope in different parts of the sky. He thought they might be scattered in space like this.

The Andromeda Galaxy
This photograph of the nearest large galaxy to our own shows the brightness of the central region compared with the spiral arms. Its pinkish colour comes from red giant stars, while most of the stars in the arms are white or yellowish main sequence objects. A dwarf galaxy lies nearby. The Andromeda galaxy contains about four times as many stars as our own galaxy.

aperture door

radio antenna

solar panels

Mirror casing

The Hubble Space Telescope

Launched in 1990, the Space Telescope is really a huge video camera, using a mirror 2.4 metres across to focus light from planets, stars or galaxies. These images are then radioed to Earth. It has been used to observe many galaxies. For example, it has discovered that the nucleus of the Andromeda galaxy is double, not single. Many people think that the Space Telescope can see further into space than other telescopes, but this is not the most important thing about it – instead, it shows far more detail.

Space telescopes

Stars often twinkle. This is due to ripples of heat in the Earth's atmosphere, which ruin the sharpness of a telescope's image. Launching the telescope into space overcomes this problem.

radio antenna

housing for cameras and detectors

The Universe is expanding?

O n the Earth we know things are in motion because we can see them move before our eyes. Galaxies are so far away that their motion cannot be seen directly at all – yet some of them are the fastest-moving objects known.

The first clue that the Universe is expanding came in the first years of this century when an American astronomer named Vesto Slipher discovered that all the galaxies he observed using a *spectroscope* showed a red shift (see below), indicating that they were moving away from us at speeds of many kilometres per second.

In 1925 the famous American astronomer Edwin Hubble began to study the red shifts of galaxies. He found that the smaller and fainter galaxies had larger red shifts than the larger and brighter ones. He eventually discovered that their distance and their velocity were linked. This meant that if the red shift of any remote galaxy was measured, its distance could be calculated. Hubble's Law offered a tape-measure to the Universe.

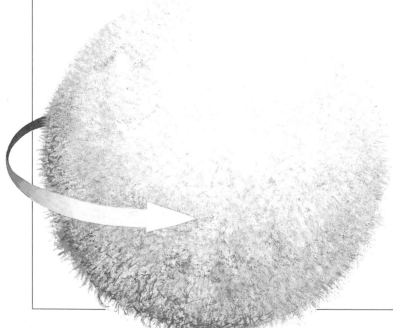

The Doppler effect

When a speeding ambulance passes by, the note of its siren falls. This is because the sound waves are compressed closer together ahead of it, and stretched farther apart behind it. Close sound waves make a higher note than more separated ones.

Blue shift and red shift

The Sun spins on its axis in 28 days, and different parts of its surface show a blue shift and a red shift. Light from the surface coming towards the Earth (the left hand edge when seen from the Earth's northern hemisphere) shows a blue shift: the right hand edge, which is moving away from us, shows a red shift. However, the effect is very small because the surface is spinning at only about 10 km/s. The most distant galaxies discovered by astronomers are flying away from the Earth at speeds of over 100,000 km/s!

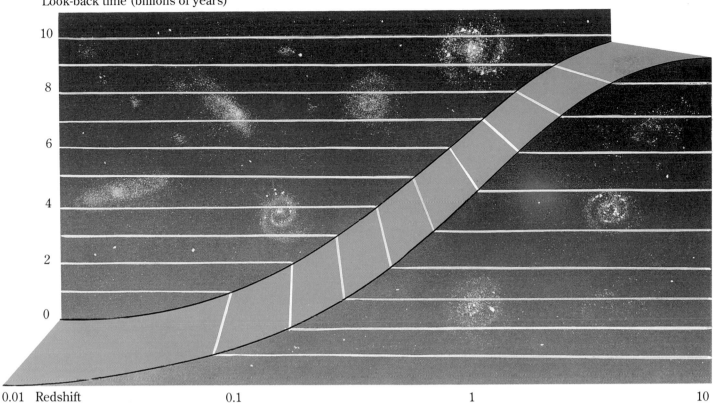

Look-back time (billions of years)

10

8

6

4

2

0

0.01 Redshift   0.1   1   10

EDWIN HUBBLE
Hubble (1889–1953) used the 2.5-metre telescope on Mount Wilson in California, then the largest in the world, to photograph galaxies and record their spectra. By 1934, after ten years' patient work, he had studied over 100 galaxies, and discovered that they seemed to be flying away from each other. In those days many astronomers (including Hubble) thought that the Universe was *static* or unchanging. His own work helped to prove that it is not.

Look-back time
How far do astronomers look back in time when they study distant galaxies? The figures along the bottom of this diagram show red-shift on a scale up to 10. The left-hand scale shows how long the light has been travelling. The most distant galaxy observed so far has a redshift of about 4, which according to the diagram means that its light began its journey about nine billion years ago – long before the Sun and planets came into existence.

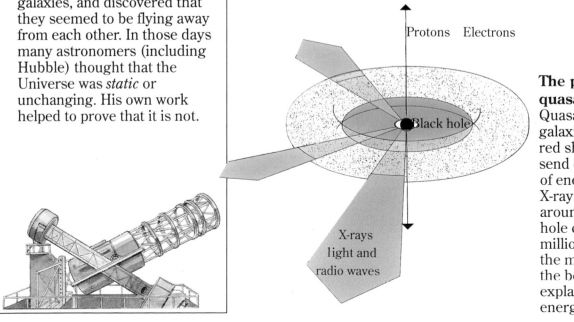

Protons   Electrons

Black hole

X-rays
light and
radio waves

The powerhouse of a quasar
Quasars are distant galaxies with the largest red shifts known. They send out huge amounts of energy, including X-rays. Gas swirling around a central black hole containing from a million to a billion times the mass of the Sun is the best way of explaining where this energy comes from.

About the beginning and end of the Universe?

The first theories about the origin of the Universe assumed that there was a creator who set everything in motion. The Biblical story of the Universe being created in six days is a good example. However, around the end of the 17th century, people began to wonder if the Universe had developed into its present state by natural change.

Isaac Newton, in 1692, suggested that if the Universe originally consisted of matter 'evenly disposed throughout a infinite space', then gravity would tend to make the matter clump together into 'an infinite number of great masses' – the Sun and the stars.

Until the present century, most astronomers accepted that the Universe was once filled evenly with material that condensed into stars and galaxies. The question of where this material came from did not arise – it just existed. But the discovery that the Universe is expanding forced them to face the question: how and when did it start expanding?

The Big Bang theory
A Belgian physicist, Georges Lemaitre, suggested in 1927 that the Universe began as a dense, hot body that expanded and cooled. Most astronomers now accept that this Big Bang happened, about 15,000 million years ago.

Imagine that these cubes are samples of a group of galaxies taken billions of years apart. The galaxies have moved further apart because the space between them has expanded, so the Universe is becoming 'emptier' as time goes by.

The Steady State theory

This theory suggested that new atoms were being created all the time, and new galaxies were forming to fill in the spaces between the old galaxies as they flew apart. In other words, the Universe had been going on for ever. The discovery in 1965 of faint radiation throughout space, apparently from the Big Bang, killed the theory.

The future

The Universe may go on expanding for ever – or it may come to a halt and collapse together again. It depends on whether there is enough material for gravity to slow down and stop the expansion, and at the moment we do not know the answer.

Penzias and Wilson

One of the most important astronomical discoveries of the 20th century was made by accident in 1965. In New Jersey, USA, Arno Penzias and Robert Wilson were trying to detect radio waves from gas clouds in space. However, their radio telescope kept picking up an unexpected 'hum'. They believed that they had accidentally discovered the last traces of the Big Bang explosion.

COBE SATELLITE

In 1990 Cosmic Background Explorer examined the faint left-over 'heat flash' from the Big Bang. This is now very cold indeed, at a temperature of $-270°C$, and the instruments on board had to be kept even colder, using liquid helium, so that they could detect it.

If there are other intelligent beings in the Universe?

How did life arrive on the Earth? Did simple living cells develop naturally out of carbon, oxygen and other elements in our planet's early atmosphere and oceans?

The starting-point is the problem. Once living cells have come into existence, biologists can explain how very simple life forms could develop into plants, animals and humans – given enough time.

If life here developed naturally, than we would expect to find life on other Earth-like planets. The question is, how common are Earth-like planets? We cannot yet observe any planets orbiting around other stars, but with millions of other stars like the Sun in our galaxy, and millions of other galaxies in the Universe, there must surely be many – and the chances are that they are inhabited.

However, the first life could have come from outside the Earth. Some meteorites contain simple *organic* molecules. One of these may have plunged into the Earth's early, warm seas perhaps 3.5 billion years ago. In this case, life on the Earth owes itself to a lucky accident.

Radio telescopes
At the present time, the best hope of discovering life beyond the Earth is to listen for radio messages being sent out by other civilisations. The Search for Extra-Terrestrial Intelligence (SETI) includes the Microwave Observing Project (MOP), which is using large radio telescopes like this one (left) at Goldstone, California, to scan the sky for radio signals.

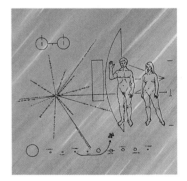

Pioneer 10
This metal panel (above) was fitted inside Pioneer 10, a space probe which passed Jupiter in 1973 and is now heading for *interstellar* space where it might one day be detected by another civilisation. The Sun and planets, and the spacecraft's path from the Earth, are shown along the bottom.

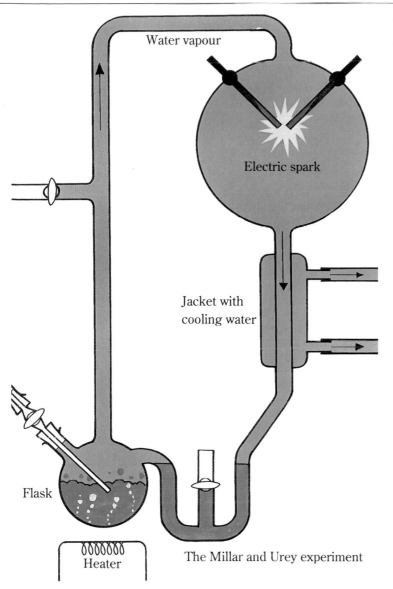

Water vapour

Electric spark

Jacket with cooling water

Flask

Heater

The Millar and Urey experiment

The start of life

All life forms are built up from microscopic living cells, and each cell contains millions of organic molecules, which are long strings of atoms linked together. These complicated molecules are in turn built up from simpler organic molecules. Could these have been created on the Earth? The answer is – possibly. About one billion years after the Earth formed, warm oceans lay under a stifling atmosphere of carbon dioxide, nitrogen, ammonia, methane, and other unbreathable gases swirling in a steamy fog of water vapour. Electric storms may have raged almost continuously – and lightning flashes are a very concentrated form of energy.

Back in the 1950s two American chemists, Stanley Miller and Harold Urey, passed electric sparks through a mixture resembling the Earth's early atmosphere and discovered that some simple organic molecules had been created. However, these early experiments and much more recent ones certainly do not prove that life did develop in this way.

The intense heat of a lightning flash can force different atoms to join together. Did life on Earth begin in a thunderstorm?

THE ECOSPHERE

If the Earth were moved closer to the Sun, or further away, could life survive on it? Every year its distance changes by about five million kilometres because its orbit is not quite circular – it is closest to the Sun in January, and most distant in July. This effect is not noticeable because the changes quickly cancel out, but if the Earth always orbited the Sun at its July distance our planet would be an icy waste. On the other hand, if it moved much closer than its January distance it would heat up into a sweltering, steamy cauldron like Venus. The ecosphere – the band around the Sun where Earth-type life could thrive – is a very narrow one.

Glossary

Atomic reactor
A power generator where energy is created by turning one type of atom into another: this also happens at the centre of a star.

Atoms
The tiny basic units of everything in the Universe, containing one or more electrons whirling around a solid nucleus.

Compressed
A solid, liquid or gas that has been shrunk into a smaller space by pressure.

Elements
The 92 different basic substances found in the Universe, from which everything else is made.

Elliptical
Another word for oval, a flattened circle. An elliptical shape can be almost circular or very long and thin.

Evolution
Gradual change over a long period of time, as animals and plants develop into different forms.

Gravity
The pulling force of stars, planets and other space bodies. The Earth's gravity pulls us down on to its surface.

Interstellar
The vast regions of space between the stars.

Luminosity
The amount of light sent out by a star: its actual brightness, not the brightness it appears in the sky.

Magnetic field
The invisible loops of force joining the two poles of a magnet.

Module
A part of a spacecraft which separates from the rest of the vehicle to carry out a special task, such as landing on a planet.

Molten
The state of a solid substance such as rock or metal when it is melted by heat.

Natural selection
Known as the 'survival of the fittest': forms of living things that suit the conditions best will survive, while the other forms may die out.

Nebula
A cloud of gas and dust, where stars are formed. The plural is nebulae.

Neutron star
The remains of a massive star after it has exploded, millions of times denser than anything known on Earth.

Organic
This literally means 'of living things': organic chemistry studies the way living cells are built up out of molecules.

Philosopher
This word means 'lover of wisdom'. Before the 19th century, a person we would now call a 'scientist' was known as a philosopher.

Physicist
Someone who studies the structure and nature of non-living objects and materials, from atoms to stars and galaxies.

Radioactive
An atom that gives out energy from its nucleus: uranium atoms are an example.

Ray
A beam of energy, which may be visible light, invisible heat, radio waves, or other kinds of radiation.

Satellite
An object in orbit around a planet. It could be an artificial spacecraft, or natural like the Moon.

Spectroscope
An instrument for studying the spectrum of a shining object such as a star, to see what it is made of.

Spectrum
The coloured band produced when a ray of light passes through a prism.

Static
Unchanging; the Universe was once thought to be static, but now it is believed to have changed or evolved since it began.

Supernova
The violent explosion of a dying star much more massive than the Sun.

Vapour
A cloud of tiny droplets of liquid formed when a gas cools: steam is water vapour.

Index

This book is due for return on or before the last date shown below.